Breaking Up With Bristol

Adele Irimiea

BookLeaf Publishing

India | USA | UK

Breaking Up With Bristol © 2024 Adele
Irimiea

All rights reserved.

Presentation by *BookLeaf Publishing*

Web: www.bookleafpub.com

E-mail: info@bookleafpub.com

ISBN: 9789360942113

First edition 2024

For My Sister

ACKNOWLEDGEMENT

Thank you to my friends. The family I have made. Dom and his lights, Natalie and her optimism, Eliza and her wildness, Steph for bringing me home, Yve for her wise smiles and my family who always keep me crazy.

PREFACE

What I have wrote has helped me deeply. I hope, if anyone out there ever does read these words, they read them with joy.

Clifton Park

Last night I dreamt of Clifton Park
I swam through rooms
Of boggy dark.

Its shadows were, in ghostly den
Frightening ghosts
As it does men

With Sally Fry
Neither her,
Nor my.

Picked up by
a churning loom
I wonder through
Room by room

As if daft
I picture sights so strange
A woman sat
Beyond a cage

Fearful now
Trevor comes up
I fear my hidings

Have come unpluck'd

Deserting encounters
Accompany me through
I ask the question
What do I do?

Stuck now.
My Bridegroom at rest
The house proposes me
Ringed up
Like a nest

The stairs unravel
Peculiar places unfold
Its different now
This is not of old

Memory, unforgiving
Dreams are latterly locked,
Wherever I am
I fear I am lost.

A Dream

When the house was unhomely
The Kettle had just boiled past ten
And the fire was ravenous
So we sat down to drink up the
Dead mice
The cat had ripped apart throughout the night.
It was thick with the stench of earth and
Downstairs lay stranger twins
With nothing in common.
I stared past the joke and got on with death
Holding a handkerchief as I laughed my two
Selves
Back upstairs
And fell back into awakening.

The Dene

Started again.
On this walk.
Gasping,
In the dene.
I make room.
An avalanche.
Like the devil's canyon.
It suppresses me.
And a child's eye's wit.
In hope and promise.
I pluck wild garlic.
And breathe back out.
The choking.
In one breath.
Breadth from park to park.
And back again.
Until it's night.

Heidelberg

5

I will return to Heidelberg,
where I cried with a fever for life and love and
hay
in a city turning over with silence and then noise
and churchly shadows
recycled round with vineyard dust
and river water

In returning
what I may
differently, find
Will be uncorrupted and pleasantly unchanged
by its summer ways and city blooms

Forever in the garden of comfort and friendship
and love lost
and eyes staring back
it exists as a yard in my mind
as a room overlooking a village
under the watch of late afternoons
and aperitifs
and wavering bees

When I return

although time grows steady upon it's whimsical
stare
I hope to find the endless promise of its
foreverness.

                    Heidelberg wait for me.

Death in a Steakhouse

Life hanging on the wall of a steakhouse in
Hexam,
I observe the glassy stare of the deer
overlooking
The people eating away.
Locked up in its wet pupils is a vision of
Another life,
Emulsified by the consciousness of death
Stunned deep into its glare.
In a coffee or two,
I'll be ready to head out.
But for this moment,
I am stuck by a mountain,
Surrounded by endless forest and life
Impaled by a bullet,
I surely failed to see.

Tarzan

Don't be silly Tarzan
Neither woman
Neither man
I am cold tonight
The moon does whip me
And the stars go out like whimpers
And your hair is short
Cut out like a little boy
Called out by a little girl
Protected by the game of jungle.

A dead sound
On the stroke of combat
The cats have gotten at me
The dog cries in the garage
From the bombs in the sky
Pretty and dissolving
Into the rolling of trees
Stretching up into our imagined skies
And joined by the hands which hold
The ropes which join
The branches falling
Between you and I

Our nails will dig it up again

And here are our mothers to tell us
And you
Tarzan
Mother of mud
Father of families
Catcher of fear
Merchant
Currency of hope
Burning brightly
I'll hold on tight
Until we must flee.

I Am The Feared Protector
Of My Inner Child

I am the feared protector of my inner child.
I wake not wanted
And gurn relentlessly
At those feeble lies.

I am the feared protector of my inner child.
Undetected
As above me, time ferments
I remain dormant and wild.

I am the feared protector of my inner child.
My quest, unhatched,
Is hard like shell
I protect like glass
I keep sane
Then erupt

For I am the feared protector of my inner child.
Look to me and you will not see
But an aging face
Who once cried silently
Against painted purple walls.

I am the feared protector of my inner child.

Your Name

Your name is that of a conqueror.
Translated back to me in a tongue-like soul.

I fail to understand it as I used to.
Like the forgotten French
Of my school days
It continues to test me

I grasp onto it,
As I do my younger self,
barely nineteen,
Who asked the right questions,
Written out in a perfect font
On that night we revelled into an intoxicating
path

I sniffed it up,
Letter by letter,
Line by line,
Racked up neatly,
And spelt out

It was like the first line of a perfect book.

I failed to read it to the very end.

Your conquering doesn't excite me anymore.
It's age-old, unpromising, demotivating,
Like you.

I still see the glory in it
But I hear the vowels like deadened rock.
And the continents hollowed out like keyholes
and fishponds.

It sounds like limbo.

It feels like not getting out to the end.

Three years to spell it out,
And saying it,
Doesn't span the whole breadth of our alphabet.

Where I once went from A to Z in one sigh
And felt the whole universe in your name.

Notes On Open Relationships

Do you think drinking French wine makes me
happy?

Happy or sad? I ask.
Sad, he tells me.
Okay.
but I'll warn you it'll break your heart.

Already broken, he replies.

To tell you the truth,
Fast women and slow orgies will ruin your life.

But how is everyone's oral health these days?
And how is the unread book in the corner of
your room?
The French one,
about a woman who lost her husband in a
motorcycling accident.

Barely hours have passed,
And I can already see the unread pages in front
of my eyes.

I don't think we want each other the way we
want us to.
Oh, lover boy.
I'd hate to be the reason you haven't found the
one.

        That's what that was about.
So, no, drinking French wine doesn't make me
happy.

What really makes me happy is when we stop
asking ourselves where it came from
And begin to ask real questions, like
do you buy a soft or hard toothbrush?
And when was it you started to use his
toothbrush after he had stopped coming?

If I say a day, you may think me heartless.
If I tell you two minutes,
you might believe me.

When will it be that I fully understand,
this thing I call lust for love.

I watched it change in front of my eyes.
When lust began to feel comfortable
And the definition of loose became boring
That's when I realised how lame they really
were.

Opening a door for love.
A performance of hedonism.

He told me he isn't hard to feed.
I wonder at her disappointment.
Thinking that they don't want each other the
way they want themselves to.

She keeps an eye on her boy's lover,
He tells me.

But he needn't worry.
I don't want him either.

I want them to get lost in Suburban Paris.

                           In truth,
I already know this will be the case.

A case like a well-packed travel bag
with electrical pouches
and space to leave behind raincoats
and a newly bought toothbrush.

Girlfriend

I am not yet comfortable with this term,
It taunts back at me,
as an old school friend would,
when mocking the packed lunch I had brought to
school.
I hate its etymological simplicity.
It's ignorance.
It's dad-joke embarrassment.
As if blending girl and friend undid its petty and
promising pleas.
I have friends who are girls
And friend who are boys
Although the latter,
Some would argue is impossible.
This is a word that does not understand my
complexities
It is arrogant to think it deserves to be said
And stated
And then unstated
And then avoided.
Does it not see how upon separation
The friend is lost
And back to girl, we become.
Somebody they used to know.

Ex girlfriend
Give me a break
Break up with me and call me a bitch
Or someone better off
Or someone who didn't understand you
Or someone who went away
Or someone who couldn't fuck your hard head

Lover may be better
I hope to one day find whatever is the word,
Whatever is the meaning
And stop staring, long into the day, out of a
window
unable to fix tea.

5 O'clock Nowhere

You chose it as you choose your wine
White for fish
Red for meat
Rose for boys
And always cheap

You picked it out
And then got weak
So had a gin
To treat the sick

You crushed it up
With sugar and lime
You told yourself
Not this time

And in response you gladly said
If not today, tomorrow instead

For nothing can truly mend the soul.
I'd rather die drunk and old.

What The Shard Told Me

O that lordy smell
Florescan and phosphorus
Along dark sides
And into rooms
I could count them all
Measured out with spoons.

At the end of that violet hour
eyes turned round
Abouts like rolling bellies
Bones cast out like years
With my back turned and fingers turning
Throbbing like two tiny lives
Remembering to touch is too
Touch is too
To touch is
Too much
Much too much

Unreal it is.
Here it racks us all up like tents
Only rocks can meet and gather here
Empty and visceral
Wrapped up nude
Mud cracked against the shore of

These roads.
These fragments
Beaten against
And along my vale

Under, under and under

Blaze

You know you can blaze your way through time,

Smoke it out.

Alarmingly rapid.

Like a great time machine.

Cheaper and more reliable than British trains.

Notes on Narcissists

A Narcissist is impatient.
A Narcissist can seem kind.
A Narcissist will tell you to hold your breath
Then knock you off your feet
And leave you to the dogs.

A Narcissist won't wait for anybody.
A Narcissist smiles at only themselves
As a projection
Into a mirror
past the point
to prove their shine.

A Narcissist is sly.
A Narcissist can be charming.
A Narcissist can give you things
So that you don't remember.
A Narcissist will apologise.
Then do it again.
And blame you.

They are a scam of humanity.

For Those I Never Met

I light a candle
When I'm in a church
I have no money
I pay in the memory
Of those I never met

Upward is Mary
Down the hatch is a bloody one

Drinking to the memory
Of those gone
drowned by a great storm.

I think.
I pray.
Every night gladly raising a glass,
Similar to the goblet which killed them.

Irony is lost in the lives that follow.

Uncle
Brother
Son

The trinity is broken.

Two brothers left.

In the name of those I never met.

In the name of the father who encourages the
same
And the children who stand by and watch
Mother who lost her brother

Name those I never met.

In candlelight
A flicker of soul fills my cup.

To my brother
Who told me he saw his face
In the burnished cremation

Of a man I never met

To a soul fevered
by intoxicating passions
Who died disbelieving there was anything
wrong

To a man
Who told me
It's not the end of the world

Like Jesus in writing
You are more real to me
As I confide in this tiny light

Only lost when I forget.
A man I never met.

Inside

In this face
In gazing back at myself
In these small lips
Curled in when
Young and cross
In these cheeks
Shaped and touched
Squished and loved
In the chin I pull at
The ears I awe at
In the teeth
Stained
And in my brain
Processing back a record
Of previous-ness
Repeated souls
Stuffed out
Pulled at
These brows like antique chests
A tongue knitted in
Wool
And thick with language
So wrong am I
An amalgamation of what came before
Yet perfectly clear

Of the feature
Here I am
Until reformed
And rebirthed
In this face
In gazing back
I'll see some more
And more

The Shore Has Broken

The wound bleeds out into graphite
The wound is weaving waves
into a tune, against harmonic shores

      how can it be
I am caught in this

     Exactness
of breaking.

     I am caught

The Way We Move

The way we are moved.
The moving body.
A wrangling,
Waving brush
Caught up against a canvas
Of air so tight
Resolute against displacement
and our unravelling edges

Life Choices

Life choices are sorrowful deeds.
In these hellos
Are whispering utterings of goodbyes
so deep
Whole universes come to annihilation

Bad Foes

What do we suppose about each other?
When we perform the way we do.
Scouting round town
(as if not really ourselves)
But whoever was picked out
By the person standing next to you.

Encore

You left the theatre before I had time.
To stand on my two feet, to tell you we nearly
touched
hearts in that ventriloquised half-dark room. I
wanted
to stem those burning waters singing over me
like tiny
pieces of glass
down my cheeks and body. At the same time, I
was
clapping
pounding the air, where the music still lay
beating the gaps of freedom where silence would
not play.
To be on the other side.
And I could see into your god skin and face.
the routine still dancing around us,
tapping me on the shoulder, turning dizzy like
Orpheus.
I re-join those cheers
following your lead.
You couldn't hear me confess.
I wasn't calling loud enough:
Don't go! Stay. Stay!

You were mouthing a smile and I still remember
your pristine
words
I wondered what you were thinking about
piercing me like those bloody red shoes, furious
as though it is shameful, I cannot be you
like rage,
pouring over us.
stretched out like limbs.
The leap of distance.
From the front row to the cheap seats
up to the gods, the only thing I could decipher -
the roar of the audience drowning my tears
the pit of the orchestra, plunging into an abyssal
silence
and the dark distance of those cool claps
between us
and the dark distance of those cool claps
between us
the pit of the orchestra, plunging into an abyssal
silence
The roar of the audience drowning my tears
Up to the gods, the only thing I could decipher -
from the front row to the cheap seats
the leap of distance.
Stretched out like limbs.
Pouring over us.
like rage,
as though it is shameful, I cannot be you

Piercing me like those bloody red shoes, furious
I wondered what you were thinking about
Words
You were mouthing a smile and I still remember
your pristine
Don't go! Stay, stay!
I wasn't calling loud enough:
You couldn't hear me confess.
Following your lead
I re-join the cheers
tapping me on the shoulder, turning dizzy like
Orpheus
the routine still dancing around us,
And I could see into your god skin and face.
To be on the other side.
Beating the gaps of freedom where silence
would not play.
Pounding the air, where the music still lay
Clapping
Down my face and cheeks and body at the same
time, I was
pieces of glass
to stem those burning waters singing over me
like tiny
hearts in that ventriloquised half-dark room. I
wanted
To stand on my feet, to tell you we nearly
touched
you left the theatre before I had time.